THE WISDOM OF THE SAINTS

INSIGHTS FROM INDIA'S GREATEST SPIRITUAL TEACHERS

DR. JAGADEESH PILLAI

|| Dedicated to all wisdom seekers around the World ||

༄

Contents

Contents

Contents

Prayer

"Om Bhadram Karnebhih Shrunuyaama DevaahBhadram Pashyemaakshabhiryajatraah SthirairangaistushtuvaamsastanoobhihVyashema Devahitam YadaayuhSwasti Na Indro VridhashravaahSwasti Nah Pooshaa VishwavedaahSwasti Nastaarkshyo ArishtanemihSwasti No Brihaspatir DadhaatuOm Shantih, Shantih, Shantih"

The literal meaning of this mantra is: OM. O Gods! Let us hear auspicious words from our ears. O reverent Gods! Let us behold propitious visions from our eyes, let our organs and body be stable, healthy, and strong. Let us do that which is pleasing to the gods in the life span allotted to us. May Indra, inscribed in the scriptures, bring us fortune! May Pushan, the knower of the world, grant us prosperity! May Trakshya, who vanquishes enemies, bestow us with blessings! May Brihaspati bring us success!
OM Peace, Peace, Peace.

About The Author

Dr. Jagadeesh Pillai is a renowned Guinness World Record holder, writer, and researcher hailing from Varanasi, also known as the abode of Lord Shiva. With a Ph.D. in Vedic Science and a range of creative ideas and achievements, he is a true polymath. He is the author of more than 100 books including Research Publications. Although his roots can be traced back to Kerala, the people of Varanasi hold him in high regard and affectionately consider him one of their own.

In 1998, Dr. Pillai was offered a job at Banaras Hindu University, but he left the position after only two months to pursue greater goals in life. He believed that in order to study Indian scriptures and engage in other creative endeavours, he needed to retire from the daily grind of working solely for money at a young age.

He started an export business from scratch, using the knowledge he had gained from a previous job in the industry. His intelligence and unique approach to business led to great success in a short period of time, earning him more in just a decade and a half than he would have in a lifetime working in a government job. Upon the passing of Dr. APJ Abdul Kalam, Dr. Pillai decided to leave the business and dedicate himself to reading, studying, researching, and experimenting.

During his tenure in the export business, Dr. Pillai traveled to over 16 countries, gaining valuable insight and experiencing the world and life in detail.

Dr. Pillai has achieved four Guinness World Records in the following subjects:

"Script to Screen" - In this record, Dr. Pillai produced and directed an animation film within the shortest time possible, breaking the previous record set by Canadians. He has also received numerous national and international awards and recognitions for this achievement.

Longest Line of Postcards - For this record, Dr. Pillai created a line of 16,300 postcards on the occasion of the 163rd anniversary of Indian Postal Day. The event also included a questionnaire about the Indian flag.

Largest Poster Awareness Campaign - Dr. Pillai designed an awareness campaign on the subject of "Beti Bachao - Beti Padhao" (Save the Girl Child - Educate the Girl Child) to achieve this record.

Largest Envelope - In tribute to the Indian Prime Minister's "Make in India" initiative, Dr. Pillai created a 4000 square meter envelope using waste paper to achieve this record.

Attempted - **70000 Candles on a 210 kg Cake** - To celebrate the 70th Indian Independence Day, Dr. Pillai attempted to light 70,000 candles on a 210 kg cake, which was recorded in World Records India.

Attempted - **Documentary on Dhamek Stupa of Sarnath in 17 Languages** - Dr. Pillai attempted to create a documentary on the Dhamek Stupa of Sarnath, dubbing it in 17 different languages. The result of this attempt is currently awaiting confirmation from the Guinness World Records.

Dr. Pillai is skilled in teaching the Bhagavad Gita, a Hindu scripture, and is popular among young people. He has helped many young people improve their lives through his motivational teachings.

In addition to teaching, he has composed and sung numerous Sanskrit Bhajans and patriotic songs.

He has also written and directed several short films and documentaries for awareness campaigns, and has volunteered with the police in both UP and Kerala to spread awareness about various issues through videos and photography.

Incredibly, he has produced and directed over 100 documentaries about the city of Varanasi, all on his own.

He has also helped and guided more than 25 boys and girls to achieve world records through creative and innovative methods. He is a multifaceted person who uses his intellect and the blessings given to him by God to excel in various areas. He is both a teacher and a student, always learning and teaching, and is able to master any subject he comes across.

He is a selfless social activist and motivational speaker who has overcome struggles and failures to become a successful and enthusiastic individual with a rich life experience.

In addition to his work with the Bhagavad Gita, he is also an efficient Tarot card reader, Astro-Vastu consultant, and a talented singer and composer. He has sung the entire Ram Charita Manas and Bhagavad Gita in his own compositions, and has sung the phrase "Lokah Samastha Sukhino Bhavantu" in 50 different languages. He is currently working on a detailed and scientific study of Vedas, Upanishads, Puranas, and the Bhagavad Gita. He has also composed and sung the Hanuman Chalisa and Gayatri Mantra in 108 and 1008 different compositions, respectively.

Awards - Four Times Guinness World Records, Winner of Mahatma Gandhi Vishwa Shanti Puraskar, Mahatma Gandhi Global Peace Ambassador, Kashi Ratna Award, Dr. APJ Abdul Kalam Motivational Person of the Year 2017, Mother Teresa Award, Indira Gandhi Priyadarshini Award, Bharat Vikas Ratna Award, Udyog Ratna Award, Vigyan Prasar Award, Poorvanchal Ratn Samman.

Preface

The wisdom of the saints has been a guiding light for seekers of truth for centuries. In India, a land rich in spiritual traditions, this wisdom has taken on many forms and has been passed down from generation to generation through the teachings of great spiritual masters. These masters, revered for their deep insights into the nature of existence, have left behind a legacy of wisdom that continues to inspire and guide seekers on their spiritual journeys.

This book, The Wisdom of the Saints: Insights from India's Greatest Spiritual Teachers," is a celebration of this rich legacy. It brings together the teachings of some of India's most influential spiritual masters, providing readers with a comprehensive overview of the insights and wisdom that these great teachers have offered. From the teachings of Adi Shankara and Ramakrishna, to the philosophy of Mahatma Gandhi and the integral yoga of Sri Aurobindo, this book offers a diverse and comprehensive look at the wisdom of India's spiritual tradition.

Whether you are a spiritual seeker, a student of philosophy, or simply someone looking to deepen your understanding of life's great mysteries, this book is for you. It provides a unique opportunity to gain insights into the wisdom and teachings of some of India's greatest spiritual masters and to explore the rich and diverse spiritual traditions that have shaped this land for centuries.

So if you are ready to embark on a journey of discovery

and to deepen your understanding of the wisdom of the saints, turn the page and begin your exploration. This book is a doorway to the rich and timeless wisdom of India's spiritual tradition and a guide to a deeper understanding of the nature of existence.

I

Significance and Contributions of Great Spiritual Masters of India

India has long been a land of spiritual masters, whose teachings have shaped the lives of countless people. From ancient times to the present day, these spiritual teachers have been revered for their wisdom and insight into the human condition. In this chapter, we will explore the life and teachings of some of India's most influential spiritual masters, and discuss the significance and contributions of these teachers to the new book, The Art of Living: The Teachings of India's Great Spiritual Masters.

The first spiritual master we will discuss is Swami Vivekananda, who is widely regarded as one of the most influential figures in modern Hinduism. Born in 1863,

Vivekananda was a disciple of the 19th-century mystic Ramakrishna Paramahamsa. He is best known for his inspiring lectures and writings, which sought to promote religious harmony and understanding between different faiths. Vivekananda's teachings focused on the importance of self-realization and the power of meditation. He also emphasized the need for social reform and the importance of service to others.

The second spiritual master we will discuss is Mahatma Gandhi, who is widely regarded as the father of modern India. Born in 1869, Gandhi was a disciple of the 19th-century mystic Ramakrishna Paramahamsa. He is best known for his philosophy of non-violence and his leadership of the Indian independence movement. Gandhi's teachings focused on the importance of truth, non-violence, and service to others. He also emphasized the need for social reform and the importance of self-discipline.

The third spiritual master we will discuss is Sri Aurobindo, widely regarded as one of the most influential figures in modern Indian spirituality. Born in 1872, Aurobindo was a disciple of the 19th-century mystic Ramakrishna Paramahamsa. He is renowned for his teachings on the power of yoga and meditation, as well as his philosophy of Integral Yoga, which emphasizes the unity of all life and the potential for spiritual transformation. Aurobindo's teachings have had a profound impact on the spiritual landscape of India and beyond, inspiring generations of seekers to explore the depths of their inner being.

Another spiritual master who left a deep impact on India

and its people is Sri Ramana Maharshi. Born in 1879, Ramana was a spiritual seeker from a young age. He is known for his teachings on self-enquiry, which involve a deep investigation into one's own self to understand the nature of reality and attain liberation. Ramana's teachings emphasize the importance of a quiet mind and self-awareness as a means to experience the truth within. He is also known for his teachings on the power of devotion and love towards the divine.

Next, we will discuss the teachings of Shri Anandamayi Ma, a renowned spiritual teacher and saint who lived from 1896 to 1982. She is known for her teachings on devotion and self-surrender, which involve surrendering one's ego and individual will to the divine. Anandamayi Ma's teachings emphasize the importance of love, compassion, and serving others as a means to attain spiritual enlightenment. She also emphasized the need for inner peace and detachment as a means to achieve happiness and fulfillment.

Finally, we will explore the teachings of Shri Mataji Nirmala Devi, a contemporary spiritual teacher and founder of Sahaja Yoga. Born in 1923, Shri Mataji is known for her teachings on spiritual awakening and self-realization, which involves awakening the dormant spiritual energy within each person. Her teachings emphasize the importance of meditation and self-awareness as a means to attain inner peace and spiritual growth. Shri Mataji also emphasized the importance of serving others and working for the betterment of society as a means to attain spiritual growth.

These spiritual masters represent just a few of the many

influential figures in India's rich spiritual tradition. Through their teachings and lives, they have inspired generations of people to seek a deeper understanding of themselves and the world around them, and to live lives of purpose, meaning, and service. The Art of Living: The Teachings of India's Great Spiritual Masters is a tribute to these exceptional teachers and the wisdom they have passed down through the ages.

1. *"The art of living is to learn from the
teachings of India's great spiritual masters
and apply them to our daily lives."*

ॐ

II

The Teachings of Adi Shankara: Understanding the Advaita Vedanta Philosophy

Adi Shankara was an 8th-century Indian philosopher and theologian who is widely regarded as one of the most influential figures in the history of Hinduism. He is credited with establishing the Advaita Vedanta school of thought, which is based on the concept of non-dualism and the unity of all existence. Shankara's teachings have had a profound impact on Hinduism and have been widely studied and discussed by scholars and spiritual seekers alike.

Shankara's life and teachings are rooted in the Upanishads,

the ancient Hindu scriptures. He believed that the ultimate truth of existence is the unity of all things, and that the individual soul is ultimately one with the divine. He taught that the path to liberation from suffering and ignorance is through knowledge and understanding of the true nature of reality. Shankara's teachings emphasize the importance of meditation, self-inquiry, and the practice of yoga. He also advocated for the practice of ahimsa, or non-violence, and the importance of living a life of service to others.

Shankara's teachings have been widely studied and discussed by scholars and spiritual seekers alike. His works have been translated into many languages and his teachings have been adopted by many spiritual traditions. His works have been studied by scholars from various religious backgrounds, including Buddhism, Jainism, and Sikhism. Shankara's teachings have also been embraced by modern spiritual seekers, who have found his teachings to be a source of inspiration and guidance.

Shankara's teachings have had a profound impact on Hinduism and have been widely studied and discussed by scholars and spiritual seekers alike. His works have been translated into many languages and his teachings have been adopted by followers from diverse cultural and religious backgrounds. Shankara's philosophy is based on the Advaita Vedanta, which is a non-dualistic system that emphasizes the unity of the individual soul and the ultimate reality, Brahman. He argued that ignorance and ego are the main causes of suffering and that through self-enquiry and devotion to Brahman, one can attain liberation and achieve a state of enlightenment. Shankara's teachings also emphasized the importance of ethics and morality, and he encouraged his followers to lead a life of devotion, service and compassion.

His works, such as the Upadeshasahasri and the Bhashyas, remain widely read and studied, and his influence can be seen in many spiritual traditions, both within and outside of India. Shankara's teachings continue to inspire and guide spiritual seekers, and his legacy continues to live on through the many disciples who have followed in his footsteps."

"The path of devotion is the path of love."

- Meher Baba

III

The Teachings of Ramakrishna and Vivekananda

Ramakrishna and Vivekananda were two of India's most influential spiritual masters. Ramakrishna was a mystic and spiritual teacher who lived in the 19th century and was known for his teachings on the path of Bhakti yoga, or the path of devotion. Vivekananda was a disciple of Ramakrishna and a renowned philosopher and spiritual leader who spread the teachings of Ramakrishna throughout India and the world.

The teachings of Ramakrishna and Vivekananda focused on the path of Bhakti yoga, which is the path of devotion to God. This path emphasizes the importance of surrendering to God and cultivating a deep connection with the divine. Ramakrishna and Vivekananda also taught the path of Karma yoga, which is the path of selfless service and action.

This path emphasizes the importance of performing actions without attachment to the results and cultivating a sense of detachment from the material world.

The teachings of Ramakrishna and Vivekananda have had a profound impact on the spiritual landscape of India and the world. Their teachings have inspired millions of people to pursue a spiritual path and to live a life of service and devotion. They have also helped to bridge the gap between Eastern and Western spiritual traditions, providing a common ground for understanding and dialogue.

The teachings of Ramakrishna and Vivekananda provide a powerful and timeless guide for living a life of purpose and meaning. They emphasize the importance of cultivating a deep connection with the divine, performing selfless service, and living a life of detachment from the material world. By following the path of Bhakti and Karma yoga, we can learn to live a life of balance and harmony, and to find true peace and joy.

In addition to these teachings, Ramakrishna and Vivekananda also emphasized the importance of mindfulness and self-awareness. They taught that through meditation and introspection, we can gain a deeper understanding of ourselves and the world around us. This self-awareness can help us to overcome negative patterns and habits, and to cultivate a sense of compassion and love for all beings.

The teachings of Ramakrishna and Vivekananda also emphasized the importance of compassion and love for all beings. They taught that we are all connected and that the well-being of others is directly linked to our own happiness and fulfillment. This principle is embodied in the Hindu concept of Vasudhaiva Kutumbakam, which means "the world is one family."

Furthermore, the teachings of Ramakrishna and Vivekananda emphasize the importance of living a life of authenticity and integrity. They encouraged people to live in accordance with their highest values and beliefs, and to cultivate a sense of inner peace and contentment. They also taught that material wealth and success are not the ultimate goals of life, but rather, that true happiness and fulfillment come from within.

The teachings of Ramakrishna and Vivekananda continue to be a source of inspiration and guidance for spiritual seekers around the world. Their teachings provide a path towards self-realization, compassion, and inner peace, and offer a timeless and universal message for living a fulfilling and meaningful life.

"Liberation is achieved by seeing the Self."

- Ramana Maharshi

৵

IV

The Teachings of Mahatma Gandhi: The Philosophy of Nonviolence and Moral Living

Mahatma Gandhi was a renowned Indian spiritual leader and political activist who is widely regarded as the father of the Indian independence movement. He was a proponent of nonviolence and moral living, and his teachings have had a lasting impact on the world.

Gandhi was born in 1869 in Porbandar, India. He was raised in a Hindu family and was deeply influenced by the teachings of the Bhagavad Gita, a Hindu scripture. He studied law in London and returned to India in 1891 to practice law.

Gandhi's philosophy of nonviolence and moral living was heavily influenced by his religious beliefs. He believed that violence was never the answer and that people should strive to live a life of truth and nonviolence. He also believed in the power of civil disobedience and peaceful protest to bring about social change.

Gandhi's teachings were put into practice during India's struggle for independence from British rule. He led a series of peaceful protests and civil disobedience campaigns that eventually led to India's independence in 1947.

Gandhi's teachings have had a lasting impact on the world. His philosophy of nonviolence and moral living has been adopted by many other leaders and activists around the world. His teachings have also been used to promote peace and justice in many countries.

Gandhi's legacy lives on today in the form of his teachings and his example of peaceful protest and civil disobedience. His philosophy of nonviolence and moral living continues to inspire people around the world to strive for a better world. His teachings are a reminder that peace and justice can be achieved through peaceful means.

Gandhi's influence extends beyond the political sphere as well. He is recognized as a spiritual leader and has been described as a saint by some. His emphasis on self-discipline, self-reliance, and the importance of moral values in one's personal and professional life have inspired people to lead a more meaningful and purposeful life.

Gandhi's life and teachings have been the subject of numerous books, films, and other forms of media. He remains one of the most recognized and revered figures in Indian and world history.

Gandhi's philosophy of nonviolence and his commitment to justice and peace continue to inspire people around the world to strive for a better world. He has left a lasting legacy that will continue to influence and inspire generations to come.

"Surrender to the divine and be free."

\- Anandamayi Ma

V

The Teachings of Sri Aurobindo: The Integral Yoga and Spiritual Evolution

Sri Aurobindo was an Indian philosopher, yogi, guru, and poet who lived from 1872 to 1950. He is best known for his teachings on Integral Yoga, which is a spiritual practice that combines the physical, mental, and spiritual aspects of yoga. His teachings focus on the evolution of the individual and the collective, and the realization of a divine life on earth.

Sri Aurobindo's teachings are based on the Vedic scriptures, which are the oldest scriptures in India. He believed that the Vedic scriptures contained the secrets of spiritual evolution and the path to enlightenment. He also believed that the Vedic scriptures were the source of all knowledge and wisdom.

Sri Aurobindo's Integral Yoga is a synthesis of various yogic practices, including Hatha Yoga, Raja Yoga, and Jnana Yoga. He believed that the practice of Integral Yoga would lead to the realization of the divine within each individual. He also believed that the practice of Integral Yoga would lead to the realization of a divine life on earth.

Sri Aurobindo's teachings emphasize the importance of self-realization and the development of a spiritual consciousness. He believed that the practice of Integral Yoga would lead to the realization of the divine within each individual and the collective. He also believed that the practice of Integral Yoga would lead to the realization of a divine life on earth.

Sri Aurobindo's teachings have had a profound and far-reaching impact on the spiritual evolution of India and the world. His philosophy of Integral Yoga has inspired countless spiritual seekers to pursue the path of self-realization and strive for the attainment of a divine life on earth. His teachings have also been instrumental in the development of a new spiritual consciousness, one that is rooted in the unity of all life and the oneness of the universe. Furthermore, his writings have provided a source of inspiration and guidance for many, helping them to find their own spiritual path and to live a life of harmony and peace.

"Spiritual awakening is the key to self-realization."

- Shri Mataji Nirmala Devi

৪৩

VI

The Teachings of Jiddu Krishnamurti: The Path of Self-Discovery and Freedom

Jiddu Krishnamurti was an Indian philosopher, speaker, and writer who is widely regarded as one of the most influential spiritual teachers of the 20th century. Born in 1895 in Madanapalle, India, Krishnamurti was raised in an environment of spiritual inquiry and exploration. He was exposed to a variety of religious and philosophical teachings, including Hinduism, Buddhism, and Theosophy.

Krishnamurti's teachings focused on the path of self-discovery and freedom. He believed that the only way to true liberation was to look within oneself and to question one's own beliefs and assumptions. He encouraged his followers to be mindful of their thoughts and feelings, and to be aware of the present moment. He also emphasized the importance of living in harmony with nature and with one another.

Krishnamurti's teachings have had a profound impact on many people around the world. His writings and lectures have been translated into numerous languages and have been widely read and discussed. He has inspired countless individuals to embark on their own spiritual journey of self-discovery and freedom.

Krishnamurti's life and teachings have been a source of inspiration for many people. His words have been a source of comfort and guidance for those seeking to find their own path in life. His teachings have been a source of hope and courage for those who are struggling to find their way in the world. His words have been a source of strength and courage for those who are striving to make a difference in the world.

Krishnamurti's life and teachings have been a source of inspiration for countless individuals. His words have been a source of solace and direction for those seeking to discover their own purpose in life. His teachings have been a beacon of hope for those struggling to find their place in the world, offering a unique perspective on life and its many complexities. His philosophy has been a source of comfort and strength for those facing difficult times, providing a sense of clarity and understanding. His words have been a source of wisdom and insight, helping to guide people on their journey of self-discovery. His life and teachings have been a source of inspiration for many, and his legacy will continue to live on for generations to come.

"Kriya Yoga is the science of God-realization."

- Paramahansa Yogananda

VII

The Teachings of Swami Sivananda: The path of Raja Yoga and Self-Realization

Swami Sivananda was a renowned spiritual teacher from India who dedicated his life to helping others find inner peace and self-realization. He was a proponent of Raja Yoga, a form of yoga that focuses on the development of the mind and spirit. Through his teachings, Swami Sivananda sought to help people find a balance between the physical and spiritual aspects of life.

Swami Sivananda believed that the path to self-realization was through the practice of Raja Yoga. He taught that the practice of Raja Yoga was a way to connect with the divine and to find inner peace. He also believed that the practice of Raja Yoga could help people to become more aware of their true selves and to develop a deeper understanding of the world around them.

Swami Sivananda's teachings focused on the importance of meditation, self-discipline, and self-reflection. He taught that meditation was a way to connect with the divine and to find inner peace. He also believed that self-discipline was essential for spiritual growth and that self-reflection was necessary for understanding one's true nature.

Swami Sivananda's teachings also focused on the importance of living a life of service. He believed that by serving others, one could find true happiness and fulfillment. He also taught that by living a life of service, one could become more aware of the interconnectedness of all things and to develop a deeper understanding of the world around them.

Swami Sivananda's teachings have been a source of inspiration for many people around the world. His teachings have helped countless individuals to find inner peace and to develop a deeper understanding of the world around them. Through his teachings, Swami Sivananda emphasized the importance of a balanced and spiritual lifestyle, incorporating aspects such as daily exercise, proper diet, meditation, and selfless service. He also stressed the unity of all religions and the importance of inner purity, love, and devotion to God. He founded the Divine Life Society in 1936, which continues to spread his teachings and serve society. Swami Sivananda's teachings are still widely read and followed today, and he is considered one of the greatest spiritual leaders of the 20th century.

"The truth is within you, seek and you will find."

- Sri Ramakrishna

VIII

The (Osho): The Path of Meditation and Self-Transcendence

Osho was born in India in the early 1930s and he spent much of his life traveling and sharing his teachings with people from all over the world. He was a spiritual teacher who taught a unique blend of Eastern and Western spirituality. He was known for his teachings on meditation, self-awareness, and spirituality, and for his criticism of organized religion.

Bhagwan Sri Rajneesh, also known as Osho, was an Indian spiritual teacher who advocated for the path of meditation and self-transcendence. He believed that the only way to achieve true inner peace and enlightenment was through the practice of meditation. He taught that meditation was the key to unlocking the power of the mind and the soul, and that it could be used to reach a higher level of consciousness.

Osho's teachings focused on the idea of self-transcendence, which he defined as the process of transcending one's ego and becoming one with the universe. He believed that this process could be achieved through the practice of meditation, which he taught as a way to connect with the divine and to experience a higher level of consciousness. He also taught that meditation could be used to gain insight into the true nature of reality and to gain a deeper understanding of the world around us.

Osho's teachings have been embraced by many spiritual seekers around the world, and his teachings have been used to help people find inner peace and enlightenment. His teachings have been used to help people find a deeper connection with their inner selves and to gain a greater understanding of the world around them. His teachings have also been used to help people find a greater sense of purpose and meaning in their lives.

Osho's teachings have been a source of inspiration for many spiritual seekers, and his teachings have been used to help people find a greater sense of peace and understanding. His teachings have been used to help people find a deeper connection with their inner selves and to gain a greater understanding of the world around them. His teachings have also been used to help people find a deeper sense of purpose and meaning in their lives.

One of Osho's most famous teachings is the concept of

"Zorba the Buddha," which is the idea that we can have the best of both worlds—the freedom and joy of Zorba the Greek and the peace and wisdom of the Buddha. This concept encourages individuals to embrace their passions and desires, while also seeking a deeper understanding of spirituality and their own inner selves.

Osho's teachings have also emphasized the importance of living in the present moment and finding joy in everyday life. He believed that happiness is not something that can be found in external circumstances, but rather it is something that is found within.

His teachings continue to inspire and influence spiritual seekers around the world. Osho's books and lectures are widely available, and his teachings have been translated into many languages. Many people consider Osho to be one of the most influential spiritual teachers of the 20th century.

"*The path of nonviolence leads to the highest truth.*"

- Mahatma Gandhi

౷

IX

The Teachings of Sri Nisargadatta Maharaj: The path of Jivanmukta and Self-Knowledge

Sri Nisargadatta Maharaj was an Indian spiritual master who taught the path of Jivanmukta, or liberation while living. His teachings focused on self-knowledge and the realization of one's true nature. He believed that the only way to achieve true freedom was to realize one's true identity as the Self, or Atman.

Nisargadatta's teachings were based on the ancient Vedic scriptures, which he interpreted in a modern context. He taught that the only way to achieve liberation was to realize one's true identity as the Self, or Atman. He believed that the only way to do this was to practice self-inquiry, or Atma-vichara. Through this practice, one could come to understand the true nature of reality and the true nature of the Self.

Nisargadatta's teachings focused on the idea of non-duality, or Advaita. He taught that the only way to achieve liberation was to realize that the Self is one with the universe. He believed that the only way to do this was to practice self-inquiry and to become aware of the true nature of reality. He also taught that the only way to achieve true freedom was to let go of all attachments and to live in the present moment.

Nisargadatta's teachings have been a source of inspiration for many spiritual seekers. His teachings have been embraced by many spiritual teachers and have been used to help people find inner peace and liberation. His teachings have been a source of guidance for those seeking to understand the true nature of reality and the true nature of the Self.

Nisargadatta's teachings have been a source of profound wisdom and guidance for countless spiritual seekers. His teachings have been embraced by numerous spiritual teachers and have been used to help people find inner peace and liberation. His teachings have been a beacon of guidance for those seeking to comprehend the true nature of reality and the ultimate truth.

Nisargadatta's teachings are centered around Advaita Vedanta, a non-dualistic philosophy that emphasizes the unity of all things and the ultimate identity of the individual self with the universal consciousness. He emphasized the importance of self-enquiry and meditation as a means of realizing this truth, and encouraged individuals to seek direct, personal experience of this truth rather than relying on belief or dogma. Nisargadatta's teachings have been recorded in the book "I Am That," which remains a popular and influential text for spiritual seekers today.

"Yoga is the union of individual consciousness with the cosmic consciousness."

- Swami Sivananda

X

The Teachings of Sri M: His Approach to Spiritual Development

Sri M is a contemporary spiritual master who has dedicated his life to helping others find inner peace and spiritual development. His teachings are based on the ancient Vedic tradition of India, and he has become a beacon of hope for many seeking spiritual guidance.

Sri M's approach to spiritual development is based on the idea that each individual is capable of achieving inner peace and enlightenment through self-reflection and meditation. He encourages his followers to practice mindfulness and to be aware of their thoughts and feelings in order to gain insight into their true nature. He also emphasizes the importance of living in the present moment and being mindful of the interconnectedness of all things.

Sri M's teachings are based on the idea that each individual is capable of achieving inner peace and enlightenment through self-reflection and meditation. He encourages his followers to practice mindfulness and to be aware of their thoughts and feelings in order to gain insight into their true nature. He also emphasizes the importance of living in the present moment and being mindful of the interconnectedness of all things.

Sri M's teachings are also focused on cultivating a sense of compassion and understanding for oneself and others. He encourages his followers to practice self-love and to be kind and forgiving to themselves and others. He also emphasizes the importance of living in harmony with nature and the environment.

Sri M's teachings are not only focused on spiritual development, but also on living a life of service and helping others. He encourages his followers to be of service to their communities and to use their talents and skills to help those in need. He also emphasizes the importance of living a life of integrity and honesty.

Sri M's teachings are a source of inspiration and solace for many seeking spiritual enlightenment. His approach to spiritual growth is rooted in the ancient Vedic tradition of India and is focused on cultivating a sense of compassion and understanding for oneself and others. Through his teachings, Sri M has become a beacon of hope and guidance for those seeking to deepen their spiritual connection.

"Freedom is the end result of self-discovery."

- Jiddu Krishnamurti

XI

The Teachings of Meher Baba: The Path of Love and Devotion

Meher Baba was an Indian spiritual master who lived from 1894 to 1969. Born in Pune, India, he gained a reputation as a spiritual teacher and guide, attracting followers from all over the world. Baba's teachings emphasize the importance of love and devotion as the foundation for spiritual growth and development.

Baba's path of love and devotion is based on the idea that the ultimate goal of human existence is to realize God-realization, or the state of being one with the divine. In order to achieve this state, Baba taught that individuals must cultivate a deep love and devotion for God. This love and devotion is not limited to any particular religion or tradition, but is instead open to all people regardless of their background or beliefs.

One of the central themes of Baba's teachings is the importance of surrender. Baba taught that in order to attain God-realization, individuals must surrender their ego and their will to the divine. This surrender involves letting go of one's attachments to the material world and focusing on the divine instead.

Baba also emphasized the importance of service to others as a means of cultivating love and devotion. He taught that by serving others with a selfless and loving heart, individuals can cultivate a deeper connection to the divine. This connection can then lead to greater spiritual growth and development.

Baba's teachings also address the nature of reality and the human experience. He taught that the material world is an illusion and that the true nature of reality is spiritual. Baba also taught that individuals are not separate from the divine, but are instead expressions of the divine in physical form.

Despite his passing in 1969, Baba's teachings continue to have a profound impact on people all over the world. Many of his followers have established communities and organizations to continue his work and share his teachings with others.

The teachings of Meher Baba offer a powerful and transformative path for those seeking spiritual growth and development. Through his emphasis on love and devotion, surrender, service to others, and the nature of reality, Baba provides a roadmap for individuals to attain God-realization and realize their full spiritual potential.

"Integral Yoga is the path of spiritual evolution."

- Sri Aurobindo

౪

XII

The Teachings of Ramana Maharshi: The Path of Self-Enquiry and Liberation

Ramana Maharshi, born as Venkataraman Iyer, was a prominent Indian sage and jivanmukta (liberated soul). He lived from 1879 to 1950 and was a key figure in the development of Advaita Vedanta philosophy. He is regarded as one of the greatest spiritual masters of modern India, and his teachings continue to inspire millions of people around the world. In this chapter, we will explore the teachings of Ramana Maharshi and their significance in the path of self-enquiry and liberation.

Ramana Maharshi was born in Tiruchuli, a small village in the Indian state of Tamil Nadu. He was an introverted child and showed a deep interest in spirituality and religious practices from a young age. At the age of 16, he had a spiritual awakening, which led him to question the nature of his own existence. This led him on a quest to understand the true self, which he referred to as "Atman" or the eternal soul.

Ramana Maharshi's teachings revolve around the idea of self-enquiry, which he believed was the path to liberation. He believed that the self was the root cause of all ignorance and that true knowledge could only be achieved by looking within. He encouraged his followers to ask themselves, "Who am I?" in order to experience the truth of their own being. This practice, known as "atma-vichara," was considered to be the most direct and effective way to achieve self-realization.

Ramana Maharshi's teachings also emphasized the importance of surrender and devotion. He believed that surrendering the ego and devoting oneself to the divine was essential for spiritual progress. He encouraged his followers to cultivate love and devotion for the divine, as this would lead to a greater understanding of the self and the universe.

Ramana Maharshi's teachings also emphasized the importance of compassion and love for all beings. He believed that true liberation could not be achieved without recognizing the interconnectedness of all things and that all beings were part of the divine. He encouraged his followers to cultivate love and compassion for all beings and to act in a way that was in harmony with the divine will.

The teachings of Ramana Maharshi continue to be a source of inspiration for those seeking a deeper understanding of spirituality. His teachings on self-enquiry, devotion, surrender, and compassion continue to be relevant and have been embraced by millions of people around the world. His legacy lives on as a testament to the power of spirituality and the transformative potential of the human spirit.

"The path to enlightenment lies in
understanding the wisdom of India's great
spiritual masters."

XIII

The Teachings of Anandamayi Ma: The Path of Devotion and Self-Surrender

Anandamayi Ma was an Indian saint and spiritual teacher who lived from 1896 to 1982. She was born in a small village in Bengal, India and was known for her teachings of devotion and self-surrender. She was an exceptional spiritual master who dedicated her life to the upliftment of others and spreading the message of love and compassion.

Anandamayi Ma's teachings revolved around the idea of surrendering one's ego and devotion to the divine. She emphasized that true happiness and peace can only be achieved by surrendering one's will to a higher power and relying on the grace of the divine. According to her, devotion should be pure and selfless, free from any expectations or desires.

One of the most important teachings of Anandamayi Ma was the practice of devotion to the divine. She believed that devotion was the key to unlocking the door to self-realization and enlightenment. She encouraged her followers to engage in devotional practices such as singing devotional songs, reciting prayers, and performing puja. By practicing devotion, one can cultivate love and devotion for the divine and ultimately attain self-realization.

Anandamayi Ma also emphasized the importance of self-surrender. She believed that self-surrender was the ultimate form of devotion, as it involved letting go of one's ego and submitting completely to the will of the divine. By surrendering one's ego and desires, one can experience the divine presence within and attain inner peace and happiness.

The teachings of Anandamayi Ma were simple yet profound. She encouraged her followers to live a life of love and compassion, and to always strive to do good in the world. She believed that by serving others, one could attain inner peace and spiritual fulfillment. She also emphasized the importance of leading a simple and honest life, free from materialistic desires and attachments.

The teachings of Anandamayi Ma are an inspiration to many people even today. Her message of love, devotion, and self-surrender continues to inspire people from all walks of life, and her teachings continue to be studied and followed by people all over the world. By embracing her teachings and practices, one can experience the path to inner peace and spiritual fulfillment.

"The key to a meaningful life is to embrace the teachings of India's great spiritual masters."

&

XIV

The Teachings of Shri Mataji Nirmala Devi: The Path of Spiritual Awakening and Self-Realization

Shri Mataji Nirmala Devi was an Indian spiritual teacher who taught the path of spiritual awakening and self-realization. She was born on March 21, 1923 in Chindawara, India and passed away on February 23, 2011. Shri Mataji was recognized as a spiritual master and a visionary who dedicated her life to serving humanity. She is revered as the founder of Sahaja Yoga, a form of meditation that aims to awaken the individual's inner spiritual potential and help them achieve self-realization.

The teachings of Shri Mataji Nirmala Devi revolve around the concept of self-realization, which she defined as a state of inner awareness where one is able to experience their own inner being and attain a deeper understanding of their connection to the divine. Shri Mataji taught that this state of self-realization can be achieved through regular meditation and the development of certain spiritual qualities such as love, compassion, and wisdom.

One of the core teachings of Shri Mataji is the idea of "Sahaja Yoga," which means "spontaneous union with the divine." According to Shri Mataji, Sahaja Yoga is a state of being where one is able to experience a deep sense of inner peace and connection to the divine. She taught that this state can be achieved through regular meditation and the development of spiritual qualities such as love and compassion.

Shri Mataji also emphasized the importance of balancing one's spiritual and material life. She taught that it was possible to live a harmonious and fulfilling life while still pursuing spiritual development. She encouraged her followers to lead a life of service and compassion, and to use their spiritual gifts to help others.

The teachings of Shri Mataji Nirmala Devi have had a profound impact on the lives of many people around the world. Her teachings on self-realization and spiritual awakening have inspired thousands of people to pursue their own spiritual journey and find inner peace. Her legacy continues to inspire people to lead a life of love, compassion, and service to others, and to achieve a deeper connection to the divine.

"The secret to a fulfilling life is to follow the teachings of India's great spiritual masters."

&

XV

The Teachings of Paramahansa Yogananda: The Path of Kriya Yoga and Spiritual Enlightenment

Paramahansa Yogananda was an Indian yogi and spiritual teacher who brought the teachings of Kriya Yoga to the West. He was born in Gorakhpur, India in 1893 and became a disciple of the great master Sri Yukteswar Giri at a young age. Yogananda's teachings revolve around the path of Kriya Yoga, which is a form of meditation and spiritual practice aimed at realizing one's true self and reaching a state of spiritual enlightenment.

Yogananda's teachings emphasize the importance of self-discovery and self-realization as the ultimate goal of human existence. He believed that by practicing Kriya Yoga and following the spiritual path, one can realize their true divine nature and experience a deep connection with the divine. Through this connection, individuals can develop a sense of inner peace, joy, and fulfillment that is not dependent on external circumstances or events.

One of the key concepts in Yogananda's teachings is the idea of the soul as a spark of divine light that is temporarily separated from its source. The goal of Kriya Yoga, according to Yogananda, is to reunite the soul with the divine source and experience the ultimate state of consciousness. Yogananda taught that the ultimate goal of life is not just to achieve material success or pleasure, but to discover one's true purpose and to become aware of the divine presence within.

Yogananda also emphasized the importance of a balanced lifestyle, incorporating both material and spiritual pursuits in one's life. He taught that it was possible to live a life of service and devotion to others while also pursuing personal growth and spiritual advancement. He believed that spiritual growth and material success were not mutually exclusive, but rather, that they could complement and enhance each other.

In the early 1920s, Yogananda came to the United States and began spreading the teachings of Kriya Yoga and the path of self-realization. Over the next several decades, he attracted thousands of followers and established the Self-

Realization Fellowship, an organization dedicated to spreading his teachings and preserving his legacy. Today, the teachings of Paramahansa Yogananda continue to influence and inspire people around the world, and his books, including "Autobiography of a Yogi", remain popular and widely read.

The teachings of Paramahansa Yogananda offer a unique and powerful approach to spiritual growth and self-realization. Through the practice of Kriya Yoga and the principles of self-discovery and self-realization, individuals can realize their true nature and experience a deep connection with the divine. Yogananda's teachings continue to inspire and guide people around the world, and his legacy remains an important part of the spiritual heritage of India.

"The journey to inner peace begins with the teachings of India's great spiritual masters."

"The way to true happiness is to heed the teachings of India's great spiritual masters."

"The path to contentment is to be guided by the teachings of India's great spiritual masters."

"The art of living is to be inspired by the teachings of India's great spiritual masters."

"The way to true joy is to be enlightened by the teachings of India's great spiritual masters."

"The key to a life of purpose is to be guided by the teachings of India's great spiritual masters."

ॐ

1. The Moments When I Met God
2. Kashiyile Theertha Pathangal
3. GURU GYAN VANI
4. Abhiprerak Gita
5. ASSI SE JAIN GHAT TAK
6. Hopelessness of Arjuna
7. The Soul and It's True Nature
8. Sense of Action (Karma)
9. Action through Wisdom
10. Action through Wisdom
11. THEORY AND PRACTICAL OF EVERY ACTION
12. LOGICAL UNDERSTANDING OF THE SUPREME
13. THE IMPERISHABLE SUPREME
14. Yatra Nishadraj se Hanuman Ghat Tak
15. Yatra Karnatak Ghat se Raja Ghat Tak
16. Yatra Pandey Ghat se Prayagraj Ghat Tak
17. Yatra Ranjendra Prasad Ghat se Dattatreya Ghat Tak
18. YaatraSindhiya Ghat se Gwaliar Ghat Tak
19. Yatra Mangala Gauri Ghat se Hanuman Gadhi Ghat Tak
20. Yatra Gaay Ghat Se Nishad Ghat Tak
21. MAA GANGA, GHATEN EVM UTSAV
22. Ganga Arti Dev Deepavali evam Any Utsav
23. Potentials of Digitalized India
24. VEDIC CONSCIOUSNESS
25. A Brief Introduction to Vedic Science
26. Kashi ke Barah Jyotirling
27. IMPACT OF MOTIVATION
28. Let's have a Milky Way Journey
29. Color Therapy in a Nutshell

90. Astrological Remedies
91. The Secret Power of Motivation
92. Secret of Developing your Inner Strength
93. The Secret Path to Motivation
94. The Art and Secret of Positive Thinking
95. The Secrets of Practicing Ethical Living
96. Indian Art and Painting
97. The Indian Herbalism
98. Bharatanatyam to Kathak
99. Exploring India's Astrological Remedies
100. The Indian Festival of Flowers
101. Indian Handicrafts
102. The Splashes of Joy – India's Colour Festival
103. The Indian Science of Astrology
104. The Indian Mythology
105. Path to Enlightenment
106. The Indian Spirituality for Children
107. Aromas of India
108. The Secrets of Healthy Relationships
109. Ancestral Ties
110. The Indian Street Food
111. Discovering America
112. The Indian Textile
113. Listening to Motivational Speeches
114. Taste of India
115. A Cultural Journey through Indian Nuptials
116. Motivational Quote for Change
117. Secret Strategies for Making Money
118. Secrets to Cultivate a Positive Mindset
119. A Tapestry of Cultures: Exploring India from Kashmir to Kanyakumari
120. Achieving Your Dreams with Resilience: Secret Strategies for Overcoming Obstacles

ॐ

CONTACT

DR. JAGADEESH PILLAI

MBA & PhD in Vedic Science

Four Times Guinness World Record Holder

Winner of Mahatma Gandhi Vishwa Shanti Puraskar and
Global Peace Ambassador

Gemology, Astro & Vastu Consultant - Spiritual Counselor

Consultant for designing World Record Ideas

Efficient Tarot Card Reader

9839093003

myrichindia@gmail.com

drjagadeeshpillai@facebook

drjagadeeshpillai@instagram
jagadeeshpillai@youtube

www. JAGADEESHPILLAI.com

|| LOKAHA SAMASTHAHA SUKHINO BHAVANTU ||

೭